DATE DUE

EXPLORING TOUGH ISSUES

Why do people take Drugs?

Patsy Westcott

RAINTREE
STECK-VAUGHN
RSVP PUBLISHERS

A Harcourt Company

Austin   New York
www.steck-vaughn.com

Published by Raintree Steck-Vaughn Publishers, an imprint of Steck-Vaughn Company

Library of Congress Cataloging-in-Publication Data
Westcott, Patsy.
Why do people take drugs / Patsy Westcott.
    p.   cm.—(Exploring tough issues)
    Includes bibliographical references and index.
    ISBN 0-7398-3231-X
    1. Drugs—Juvenile literature.
    [1. Drugs.]
    I. Title. II. Series.

Printed in Italy. Bound in the United States.
1 2 3 4 5 6 7 8 9 0 05 04 03 02 01

Picture acknowledgments

The publisher would like to thank the following for their kind permission to use their pictures: Eye Ubiquitous/ James Davis Travel Photography 24/ Paul Seherut 27 (bottom); Angela Hampton Family Life Picture Library 5, 26; Hodder Wayland Picture Library 14 (left), 21 (top and bottom), 29, 39, 43 (top)/ Jeff Greenberg 9/ APM Studios 11/ Chris Fairclough 21/ Zak Waters 30; Impact/ Andy Johnstone 4/ Steve Parry 17/ Rupert Conant 27; Panos/ Adrian Evans 12/ Crispin Hughes 23/ Trygue Bolstad 25/ Gareth Wyn Jones 28 (top)/ Daniel O'Leary 33/ Giacomo Pirozzi 36, 40; Photodisc (*cover*); Photofusion 18,/ Crispin Hughes 35/ Mark Campbell 18, 45; Popperfoto (*title page, contents, bottom*), 6, 7, 8, 13, 14 (right), 19, 20, 22, 31, 32, 34, 38 (bottom), 41, 42, 43 (bottom), 44; Science Photo Library 6 (top and bottom); Skyjold 10, 15, 38 (top); South American Pictures/ Tony Morrison 5 Artwork on page 16 by Rachel Fuller.
Thanks to the Health Development Agency for its kind permission to print the leaflets on page 37.

Contents

1. What are drugs?

What do you think drugs are?

When you hear the word drugs, what kind of picture comes into your mind? Do you imagine people in a doorway injecting themselves with a syringe? Do you picture people dancing at a club or party after taking Ecstasy (E)? Do you think of someone lighting up a cigarette or drinking a glass of beer? If you take a painkiller for a headache, is that taking a drug? And when you drink a can of cola are you a drug taker?

Many people find out what they know about drugs from watching movies and TV or by reading newspapers and magazines. Because of the ways drugs are presented in the media, people often think bad things about drugs. But drug taking is something almost everyone does all over the world.

▼ *People smoking marijuana in one of Amsterdam's many coffee shops*

In Western countries, like the United States and the UK, most adults drink coffee or tea, which contain the drug caffeine. Many people smoke cigarettes, which contain the drug nicotine, or drink alcohol. A growing number of people take prescribed medicines and herbal remedies that are available over the counter. In some countries, drugs such as cannabis are allowed. In South American countries such as Peru and Bolivia, some Indians chew coca leaves, from which cocaine is made, to help them cope with demanding work.

▲ Tablets used to treat headaches and other minor aches and pains are drugs.

"Every society has its own drugs. People have always used drugs...(and) we all take drugs in one way or another...."
Forbidden Drugs,
Philip Robson

▲ Indians in the highlands of Peru selling coca leaves. Chewed or made into a tea, the leaves are also a source of vitamins.

What are drugs exactly?

Drugs are chemicals, or substances, that change the way your body works or affect the way you think, feel, or behave. Many of these chemicals come from natural products. For example, wine comes from grapes and marijuana comes from the leaves of a plant called *cannabis sativa*. Other drugs, like amphetamines, are made in laboratories.

Some drugs are medicines. You can get them when the doctor writes you a prescription or when you buy them over the counter at the supermarket or drugstore. Medical drugs are used to treat or prevent disease. Drugs known as vaccines are often given to keep people from getting serious diseases like polio, tetanus, diphtheria, whooping cough, and measles. This is called immunization.

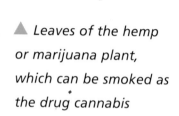

▲ *Leaves of the hemp or marijuana plant, which can be smoked as the drug cannabis*

Other drugs are in everyday drinks or food. Coffee contains caffeine, a drug that makes you feel more active and alert. Chocolate, tea, cola, and many other soft drinks also contain caffeine. Alcohol is another common drug that is easily available.

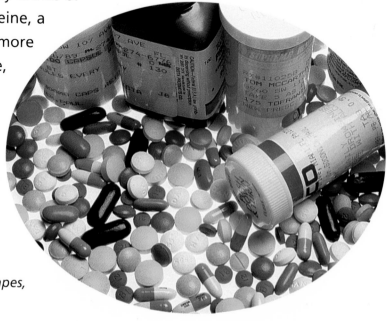

▶ *Many drugs are medicines. They come in many colors, shapes, and sizes.*

6

Cigarettes, cigars, and pipe tobacco all contain nicotine, another drug. Tobacco is made from the dried leaves of the tobacco plant. Marijuana is another drug that can be smoked.

▼ *These Cambodian street children are sniffing glue.*

Some drugs are found in ordinary household substances like glue, or butane gas, which is used to fill cigarette lighters. These drugs are manufactured in laboratories and sold in all sorts of stores and supermarkets.

```
            Fact:
Herbal medicines are becoming more popular.
  You can buy them in health food stores,
  supermarkets, and drugstores. Because they
 are made from plants and herbs, many people
   think of them as more "natural" than pills
     and tablets, but they contain active
  ingredients that, like other drugs, change
         the way your body works.
```

What are the laws about drugs?

All countries have laws for drugs. In most Western countries, drugs like caffeine, alcohol, and nicotine are legal. In many of these countries, other drugs, such as cannabis, Ecstasy, and cocaine, are illegal. Legal drugs mean there is no law to stop you from taking the drug. Illegal drugs mean the law does not let you take them. Different countries have different punishments for possessing or using illegal drugs that range from fines to imprisonment. The law is hardest on drug dealers who sell drugs to other people.

When people talk about drugs what they often mean are illegal drugs. Other names that are sometimes used to describe illegal drugs are "illicit" drugs, "street" drugs, and "social" drugs.

Religion often affects what people think about drugs. For instance, alcohol is forbidden in the Koran, the Muslim holy book. In parts of the world such as Pakistan, where people practice the Muslim religion, alcohol is illegal. Smoking marijuana is part of the Rastafarian religious ceremony, although Rastafarians disapprove of other drugs, including alcohol. In the Jewish religion, there are rules about wine and the use of any substance that can damage your health.

▼ *A Rastafarian in South Africa lighting a pipe containing marijuana*

FACT:
Around 10 million people in the UK have tried an illegal drug. Just think, that's about the number of people who live in London. Two million of these people use them regularly.
ISDD, UK Drug Situation 1999

Body builders use anabolic steroids to build their muscles, but anabolic steroids are banned in sports competitions.

Legal drugs, such as nicotine or alcohol, often have laws for under-age users, but adults can make their own informal rules about when they use them. For example, most adults save alcohol for the evening after work to help them relax. Other drugs, such as anabolic steroids, which are used by body builders and athletes, are banned in sports competitions. The rules and laws about drugs depend on all sorts of things like who you are, how old you are, what you believe, and where you live.

2. What do drugs do?

What are the effects of drugs?

People who drink tea, coffee, and alcohol or smoke cigarettes often use them because of the way they make them feel. For example, they might have a glass of wine or beer after work to help them to relax.

Drugs can have all sorts of different effects. Some drugs mainly affect the body. For example, antibiotics prescribed by doctors to cure some infections work by destroying harmful germs in the body.

Other drugs mainly affect the mind. The chemicals in them act on the brain, changing the way people who have taken them feel or the way they behave. Sometimes, these effects are pleasant. Ecstasy and cannabis can boost the pleasure people get from dancing or listening to music. Sometimes, the effects can be less pleasant. Ecstasy and cannabis can make people feel anxious and panicky, too.

▶ *People often take drugs, such as cannabis, for the short-term effects.*

"I don't feel human in the morning until I've had at least one cup of coffee. I sit at the kitchen table and, after about a quarter of an hour, I start to feel more energetic and then I make breakfast. If I'm feeling tired, I sometimes need another cup to get me going." *Larry, 20*

The effects of drugs can be divided into short-term effects and long-term effects. Short-term effects are changes that happen more or less immediately after taking a drug and don't last long. Long-term effects usually happen when people take a drug regularly over a longer period of time. Sometimes these can cause changes to the body and/or the mind that can be damaging to health and well-being.

▼ *People who smoke cigarettes often enjoy smoking with friends after a meal.*

Different drugs and their effects

Many illegal drugs change the way the mind and body work. They can create pleasant feelings, and people take them because they want to get those effects.

There are four main groups of illegal drugs that create different kinds of effects. The main drug groups are depressants, stimulants, sedatives, and hallucinogens. These drugs might affect different people in different ways but, in general, most people will experience a similar reaction.

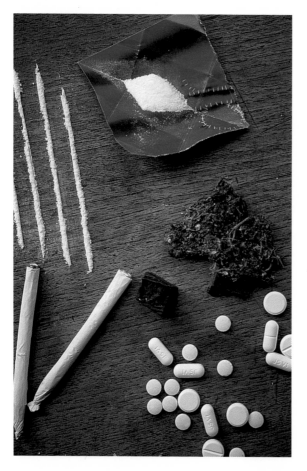

FACT:
The use of solvents is especially common among the world's estimated 100 million street children. In Guatemala nine out of ten street children are thought to be dependent on paint thinner and glue.
Andrew Tyler,
Street Drugs

◀ *Different kinds of illegal drugs. Top and top left: cocaine. Center: cannabis resin blocks. Below left: cannabis cigarettes. Below right: Ecstasy tablets.*

1. Depressants

Depressant drugs slow you down. These make you feel less anxious and more relaxed. Often these make you drowsy. Alcohol, sleeping pills, glue, and butane gas are all depressant drugs.

▼ People who go to dance parties may take stimulant drugs like Ecstasy to make them feel energetic.

2. Stimulants

Stimulant drugs make you feel awake and energetic. Stimulants keep you from feeling hungry. However, once the effects have worn off you feel hungry and very tired. Stimulants include caffeine, nicotine, amyl nitrite and butyl nitrite (poppers), cocaine and crack cocaine, Ecstasy, amphetamines (speed), and anabolic steroids.

"It didn't seem to have much effect at first but then I noticed that we were all getting chattier and I felt quite excited and cheerful. We talked our heads off and I felt really energetic. I spent all night on the dance floor."

Oli, 18, talking about Ecstasy

3. Sedatives

Sedative and pain-killing drugs make you feel sleepy, take away pain, or cause unconsciousness. Many of these drugs are called opiates because they are manufactured from the opium poppy. These drugs include heroine, morphine, which is often used to control severe pain in cancer patients, and codeine, which can be bought over the counter for headaches, stomach upsets, toothaches, and other pains.

▲ *Some sedative drugs, like codeine, used to treat pain, can be bought without a prescription in drugstores.*

▶ *This Vietnamese man is getting ready to smoke opium. Opiate drugs like morphine, codeine, and heroin are made from opium.*

case study · case study · case study · case study · case study

Jo was 17 when she first tried magic mushrooms. She tried them with a group of friends. This is how she described her experience:

"I became convinced that the wax in the lava lamp was looking at me so I had to put my hood up. I thought it was odd and funny but at the same time I felt that putting my hood up was the safest thing to do. My friends thought it was really funny. We went to a club and I felt absolutely fine so long as I hid my face in my boyfriend's shoulder. At one point he needed to go to the toilet and had to put me on someone else's shoulder while he went! Whenever anyone asked if I was OK I said 'Yes, fine.' I liked the feeling of everyone milling around and hearing all the music as long as I was hiding on his nice safe shoulder."

4. Hallucinogens

These are drugs that alter the way people see, feel, hear, or sense things. They may cause hallucinations, which means experiencing strange sensations, seeing things in a different or unusual way, or seeing, hearing, or feeling things that aren't really there. These drugs are called hallucinogens. Hallucinogens include LSD (acid), magic mushrooms, Ecstasy, and cannabis.

▲ *Hallucinogenic drugs change the way people feel, hear, or sense things.*

Drugs affect everyone in different ways

No two people react in exactly the same way to the same drug. Even if people have taken a drug before, they don't always react in the same way every time they take it. It depends on the circumstances people are in when they take the drug, how they are feeling before they take it, and what they want or expect to happen. It also depends on the people they are with and whether those people make them feel relaxed or nervous.

The precise effects drugs have depends on all sorts of different things. The effects of any drug will depend both on the drug itself—what chemicals it contains, how pure it is, how it is taken, how much is taken—and whether the person has taken the drug before. Finally, it depends on the person taking it, the mood the person is in, and how his or her body deals with it.

▼ *Ecstasy can make you feel happy and eager to dance. It can also make you feel confused or very sick.*

People who take a drug such as cannabis find that they react differently to the drug each time they smoke it. Here are some different people's experiences of smoking cannabis:

"When I've smoked a joint I find comedy absolutely hilarious. Maybe it's not really that funny, though."

Jade, 18

"Once in India I smoked some marijuana with some other travelers I met. I felt sick and dizzy and became frightened and panicky. I thought I was dying. I think it was stronger than the stuff I'd smoked at home."

Jude, 23

"Sometimes when I smoke I become frozen with fear. This usually happens when I'm smoking with people I don't know well. I no longer seem to understand what people are talking about and suspect they are talking about me."

Tobe, 32

◀ *People often have different experiences each time they smoke marijuana.*

17

3. Who takes drugs and why?

Making decisions about drugs

When it comes to drug taking, experts have discovered there are four main groups of people. There are many people who do not want to take illegal drugs at all. These people are called abstainers. Other people decide to find out about drugs by taking them. They might try out drugs and use them just for a short time, or they might only try them once or twice. They are called experimental users.

"When I go out on Friday or Saturday I take Ecstasy or coke. I've discovered this hardly ever makes me feel really ill the next day and makes me much livelier than alcohol, which makes me feel heavy and hungover the next day. Other times I drink red wine because I like its taste."

Jayne, 21, social drinker

◄ *Social or recreational users often take drugs on weekends for fun.*

Social or recreational users are another group of people. They use drugs more regularly and usually for fun—often on weekends. They often think they know quite a lot about the drug or drugs they choose to use, and take care what they use, how much they use, and how often they use them. The last group is people who have problems with drugs. These people may find it hard to control their drug use. They find it hard to stop taking the drug. They may be dependent on it.

When people use any sort of drug, such as cannabis, Ecstasy, or heroin, they often use it more at some times than others. The drugs they take vary depending on who they are mixing with and other things that are going on in their lives. Some people take drugs like amphetamines and Ecstasy when they go out to clubs because the drugs make them feel more energetic and friendly.

◀ *People who have problems with drugs, like this young woman who is injecting heroin, cannot control their drug use.*

Why take drugs?

So why do people take illegal drugs? The reasons are as different as the people who take them. Some people use drugs to make them feel more confident and less shy. Some people use them because they think it makes them seem more grownup and sophisticated or independent. Many people use them because they enjoy the effects. They like feeling happy, energetic, giggly, or however the drug they have taken makes them feel. Some people do it to be fashionable—drug taking often goes with wearing particular clothes, dancing, or listening to certain kinds of music.

Other reasons people take illegal drugs:
♦ a wide range of drugs may be easily available locally
♦ because they are bored and taking drugs is something to do
♦ to feel part of the crowd—their friends are taking drugs and they want to join in
♦ to shock or to rebel—to do something teachers, parents, and other people disapprove of
♦ because people think drugs will help them cope with problems—such as having no money or having no job

▲ *Liam Gallagher, lead singer of the band Oasis is often linked with drug taking. Now, however, he says he is drug-free.*

case study · case study · case study · case study · case study

Johnny, a student, and some friends celebrated another friend's birthday at a nightclub. One friend took Ecstasy almost every weekend and Johnny's friends wanted to try it, too. They kept laughing and saying, "Shall we? Shall we?" and, "Are you going to?" to Johnny. Johnny felt nervous and kept saying, "I don't know." But eventually his curiosity won and he said, "OK." They all felt very excited.

Later, when they all went onto the dance floor, Johnny just wanted to dance and dance. He liked the feelings it gave him and he liked everyone, including total strangers!

The next day Johnny felt very tired and stayed in bed all day. He was glad he'd tried Ecstasy, but one of his friends didn't like it, so Johnny was unsure whether he'd do it again.

▲ *Some people take drugs because they want to appear grownup and independent.*

▶ *People may take drugs because they would rather feel part of the gang than left out.*

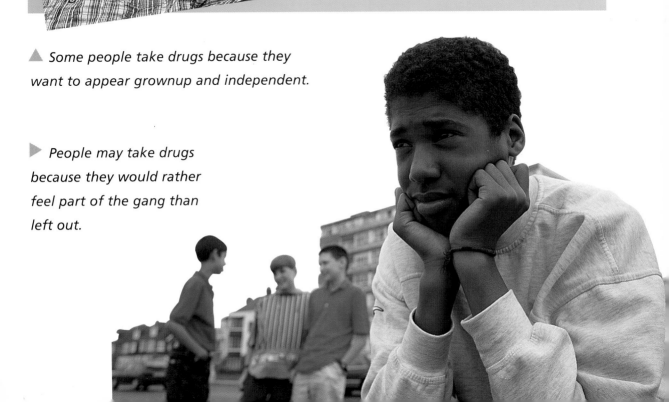

Drugs on the increase

All over the world, illegal drug taking is on the increase. Agencies set up to help people who have problems with drugs are busier than ever before, and reports show that more and more people are trying drugs at younger ages.

► *Customs officers in France seizing a haul of Ecstasy. Drugs are big business and are carried all over the world hidden in trucks, boats, and planes.*

> FACT:
> Worldwide, 141 million people take cannabis every year—that's 2.5 percent of people living in the world today. About 30.2 million take amphetamine-type drugs, 13.3 million take cocaine, and 8 million take heroin.
> Global illicit drug trends, UN Office for Drug Control and Crime Prevention, 1999

There are many different reasons for the increase in drug taking. Poor housing, lack of jobs, and poverty in many parts of the developing world where drugs are grown mean that farmers who grow crops like coca, opium, and marijuana are able to make money to feed themselves and their families.

These street children in Nairobi, Kenya, hang around garbage dumps sniffing glue. All over the world, drug taking is on the increase.

The chemicals used to make drugs are also cheap and readily available now. There are more laboratories and means of making drugs than ever before. There are also more trucks, boats, and planes to carry drugs from one part of the world to another.

Drugs have become big business. The drug trade is worth more than $60 billion a year and accounts for 8 percent of world trade—about the same as the gas and oil industries together.

```
        FACT:
   Colombia's yearly
   income from illegal
   drugs is said to be
      worth more than
       $480 million.
The Daily Telegraph, London
        6.10.99
```

4. Drugs and you

Side effects of drugs

Taking risks, experimenting with new things, and wanting to change the way we feel are part of life. We all take some risks in our everyday lives, and most of the time the risks don't harm us. Some people who use drugs come to no harm either. However, all drugs, including caffeine, alcohol, tobacco, and drugs used as medicines, can have adverse effects—these are dangerous or unpleasant things that happen as a result of taking the drug. When a drug is used as a medicine these adverse effects are known as side effects.

Some of the harmful health effects that drugs can have happen immediately. Others may develop over a period of time.

▶ *Taking risks and experimenting with new things, like snowboarding, are normal parts of life.*

Health effects of drugs include:

♦ Caffeine can cause the heart to beat faster. Although this is normally harmless, a few people have dangerous reactions after drinking just one cup of coffee.

♦ Large doses of the painkiller aspirin taken over a long period of time can make the

▲ This girl from Bombay collapsed after sniffing glue. Solvents can stress the heart and cause heart attacks.

lining of the stomach bleed. People who take painkillers, like aspirin, every day to cure headaches, may actually develop headaches caused by the painkiller.

♦ Smoking cigarettes over many years is linked to lung problems and heart disease.

♦ Regularly drinking too much alcohol can lead to high blood pressure and an increased risk of strokes. People can also become dependent on alcohol. Long-term effects include damage to the heart and the liver.

♦ Solvents can stress the heart and cause heart attacks.

♦ Long-term use of marijuana can cause forgetfulness.

♦ Ecstasy can cause overheating and dehydration, which can cause death.

♦ Heroin can cause constipation and breathing problems.

Drugs and your health

When doctors prescribe medicine, they are careful to weigh all their likely effects on the person's health and prescribe exactly the right amount for that patient. However, it is more difficult for people who take illegal drugs because it is hard to know what they contain or how much to take.

A serious risk with illegal drugs is taking an overdose—that is, taking so much of a drug that the body cannot cope with it. An overdose of alcohol, sleeping pills, or heroin can kill. With some drugs, such as heroin, crack cocaine, and Ecstasy, there is also the risk of impurity. Illegal drugs are often mixed with other substances to make them go further. The person taking the drug has no way of knowing how strong the drug is and exactly what's in it.

▲ *An overdose is a serious risk when people take depressants or sedatives.*

People who inject drugs also take risks when they share needles. Blood infections such as HIV or hepatitis C can quickly be passed from user to user.

FACT:
In the last six months of 1998, 695 people in England and Wales died from drug-related deaths.
Almost three quarters of these (74.2%) were males under 45 years of age.
Drug-related deaths as reported by coroners in England and Wales, July-December 1998.

Illegal drugs can be especially risky for people who have existing health problems. If somebody already has a problem with his or her heart, for example, then a stimulant drug may cause a heart attack. Ecstasy can also cause seizures in people with epilepsy. Illegal drugs, such as heroin, also have effects on unborn babies. Drugs pass from pregnant mothers to the unborn baby. Some babies are born dependent on heroin.

▼ *When people who inject drugs share needles, there is a risk of passing on serious infections such as hepatitis C or HIV.*

▲ *This drug user from Poland has HIV. Drug use can often lead to other problems like HIV.*

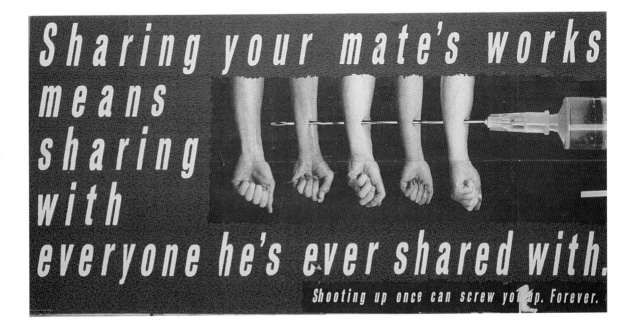

Sharing your mate's works means sharing with everyone he's ever shared with.

Shooting up once can screw you up. Forever.

How drugs affect your life

As well as harming the body, drugs also put the user in dangerous situations. For example, drugs affect the time it takes people to react. People can become drowsy and confused. This makes driving a car, operating a machine, and crossing the street dangerous, even if the person thinks he or she feels OK.

"My first conviction was for stealing car stereos to get money to buy butane gas. I was on six cans a day."

Anita, 28

◀ *Drug takers on an unused train line in Zurich, Switzerland. The people in this picture have made drugs their lives. They surround themselves with other drug takers and share needles.*

case study · case study · case study · case study · case study

Natasha, a student aged 21, first took Ecstasy in a nightclub. Lots of her friends used it and she wanted to try it too. She enjoyed its effects and soon she was going to nightclubs and taking Ecstasy several times a week. Natasha didn't have enough money to pay for going to nightclubs so often and buying Ecstasy. She borrowed money from friends, and she sold her camera, her stereo, and her bike. When that money ran out, she started stealing CDs, videos, and clothes from stores, which she also sold to get money to buy Ecstasy. One day, Natasha was caught shoplifting on a store's security camera. She was arrested and had to go to court. She was fined, and her story was in the local newspaper. Natasha felt very ashamed because people she knew read about her.

▲ *Taking illegal drugs can lead some people to commit crime.*

Drugs can also affect people's moods and can make them aggressive. People who are involved with drugs often mix with other people who are involved with drugs. It can be a violent and dangerous world with people taking drugs in derelict buildings or near train stations. It is a world where it is easy to get into trouble with the police and face the risk of being arrested, fined, and even sent to prison. This can affect schooling or work.

5. What is drug dependency?

What does dependency mean?

One of the dangers of some drugs is dependency. Some people become physically dependent on drugs—this means their bodies cannot work properly without the drug, and they feel sick if they do not have it. Drugs that can cause physical dependence include nicotine, heroin, tranquilizers, and alcohol.

It is possible to become psychologically dependent on many other things—chocolate, shopping, playing games on the computer, or gambling. Whatever a person becomes dependent upon, it starts to be more important than anything else in life.

People who become dependent on drugs often find that it affects the way they live their everyday lives. Their friends may be mostly other people who are dependent on drugs. This can sometimes make it hard if they want to stop taking drugs. They may find it difficult to find or keep jobs or to find somewhere to live.

▲ It is possible to become psychologically dependent on many pleasurable things —even chocolate.

FACT:
Nine out of ten young people living
on the streets are thought to be using one drug
or another. About 40 percent of the people who
are unemployed report using a drug within the
last year. Half of the people going to prison
are thought to be using drugs regularly. Most of
them have problems with drug use.
ISDD, The Drug Situation 1999

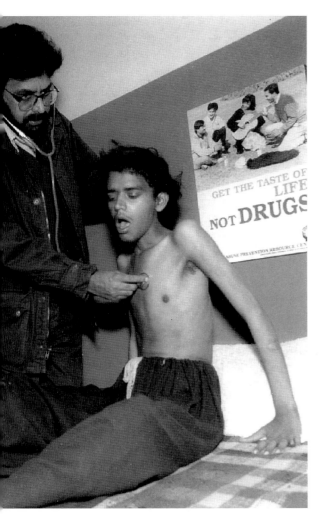

They may have money problems—especially if they don't have jobs or anywhere to live. They may break the law by stealing things from stores to get the money they need to pay for their drugs. They may sell their bodies for sex or sell drugs to other people to get money.

Their health may also suffer. Some drugs take away an appetite and keep people from feeling pain and other discomforts. People who are dependent may not look after themselves properly, and they become more likely to catch diseases.

◀ *This Pakistani boy is a heroin addict. People who become dependent on heroin often neglect their health and are more likely to become ill.*

How does dependency start?

All over the world, the number of people who have problems with drugs is reported to be increasing. These people come from many different backgrounds. The way they think, the way they feel, and the ideas they have about the world we live in are unique, too. In short, each one is an individual.

▶ *Two drugs users in Vancouver, Canada. The number of people who have problems with drugs is increasing all over the world.*

"After they've left school and find out there's nothing for them to do, they soon find out they can only stay in bed in the morning for so long. They can only watch TV for so long. They get so depressed and somebody comes along and says, 'Well, just try this,' and they say, 'Oh, I'm not touching that, it's addictive. Well, perhaps I'll just have it once but I won't have it any more.' They take it, then, suddenly, for five or six hours...the world is as they want it to be. Then they've got to come down and face life again. Two months might go by, and they might start getting depressed again and they think, I'll just have a bit of heroin to get me out of this, and that's how it goes on."

from Parents Against Drug Abuse, *quoted in Andrew Tyler,* Street Drugs

People develop problems with drugs for different reasons, but many do have some experiences in common. Many are poor and live in bad housing. Many are homeless or come from areas where finding somewhere to live or getting a job are difficult. Many have experienced other difficulties in their lives, such as problems at home or school. Sometimes, they have been brought up in families where there are many problems, such as parents who already have alcohol and drug dependency. Sometimes, they have not done well in school, or school was a miserable time for them because of bullying.

▶ *People who have problems with drugs often have bad starts in life. Homelessness, or coming from a poor background, like this street boy in Lisbon, Portugal, might lead to drug problems.*

What does it feel like?

Many people who have problems with drugs have poor opinions of themselves. They often don't like themselves very much and they may believe they are not as smart as other people or as capable of getting on in life and achieving things. People who have these beliefs are said to have low self-esteem. But do these people have low self-esteem before they become dependent on drugs? Or has becoming dependent on drugs made them feel bad about themselves?

There are all sorts of terms used to describe people who have problems with drugs. Junkie, addict, drug misuser, and drug abuser are some of them. However, many people who use illegal drugs do not like these terms, because they seem to criticize what sort of people they are. The term many prefer is a person who has problems with drugs.

▼ *A street child in Rio de Janeiro, Brazil, sniffing glue. Taking drugs can help people blot out the difficulties of their lives— at least for a short time.*

case study · case study · case study · case study · case study

Jack is 25. As a child, his parents moved around a lot, and he never quite felt he belonged. At school he felt angry, anxious, and misunderstood. He started skipping classes. At 14, Jack began sniffing solvents and taking cough medicine with two friends at school. Taking drugs made everything feel better. He no longer felt angry, anxious, and misunderstood. Later, he started smoking marijuana and using amphetamines and LSD. At 15 he was expelled from school.

After leaving school Jack made friends with more people who were taking drugs including heroin. Jack wanted to try heroin too and, at 17, he did. At first, he thought heroin was wonderful. It made him feel safe and warm and calm. But one day when he didn't take any heroin, he felt very ill. Jack realized he was dependent on heroin. It was a terrible shock. He didn't want to be dependent on heroin. He decided it was time to seek help for his problem.

▶ *This young man has problems with drugs. He's also homeless and finds it difficult to ask for help.*

35

Help for people with problems

Many people who are dependent on drugs want to stop taking them. Just like other people, they want to have a job....a home, a family, and have fun without being dependent on drugs.

In most countries there is a range of help, such as help lines and specialist services, which has been specially developed to offer advice, information, and counseling to people who have problems with drugs.

People also need the help and support of their friends and families. They need to feel listened to and that other people understand how they feel. They need to be encouraged to feel better about themselves and not to fear that other people are talking about them or criticizing them. Above all, they need to feel that they can do something about their problems.

▲ *This Zambian girl is talking to a counselor about her drug taking.*

Sometimes, people need medical help to enable them to stop being physically dependent on drugs. Doctors, and others who work with people who have become dependent on drugs, know that, although physical dependency can be broken quickly, it can sometimes take a long time to break a psychological dependency. The first step is to recognize that there is a problem.

People who succeed in breaking their dependence on drugs usually manage to find other things to interest them and other ways to have fun. This may be a new boyfriend or girlfriend, a new job, or even another "addiction," such as dancing or sports, less damaging to their health.

FACT:
Many people believe that people who use drugs can be helped best by other people who use or have used drugs and who know about them from personal experience. There are many "self-help" groups run by people who once had drug problems themselves.

◀ Many drug information leaflets are published in countries all around the world. Having accurate information about drugs can help people make their own decisions about using drugs more safely.

6. What do people think about drugs?

Attitudes toward illegal drugs

What people think about drugs depends very much on who they are, where they live, what they know about drugs, their own experiences, and their ideas about the world.

Because we are all individuals, we see the world in different ways. The way we think about things often depends on the experiences we have had, as well as what we have learned from parents, friends, and teachers. People often have different ideas about illegal drugs and ways to help people who use them.

▲ *Parents' attitudes about illegal drugs can be very different than your own. Talking about your opinions may help.*

◀ *People's ideas about drugs often come from their experiences. These boys in Glasgow, Scotland, are lighting candles at the start of a vigil against drug dealing after a local boy died from taking heroin.*

"I can't believe now how much of my life I wasted doing nothing."
Daisy, a former heroin user

"If I ever caught my son taking drugs I'd throw him out of the house."
Charles, parent

"Drug use can provide a sense of belonging and a chance to meet those with similar problems."
Deborah Allen, lecturer

"Just belonging to a group doesn't make me feel that I have to do something I don't want to do, like taking drugs....But if I listen to the same music and wear the same type of clothes as people in a group who take drugs, it is more than likely I will be labeled as a drug user...."
Roxanne Shepherd, 18, quoted in Drug Education Matters, *Spring 1999*

When people are frightened about drugs it is sometimes because they don't know much about them. Things you don't know about are always more scary than things you do know about. Having accurate facts about things can help take away fear because it means you know what you are facing and can plan how to deal with it.

▼ *Many people get their ideas about drugs from what they read in magazines and newspapers. Everyone has different ideas about drugs gained from their families, teachers, and friends.*

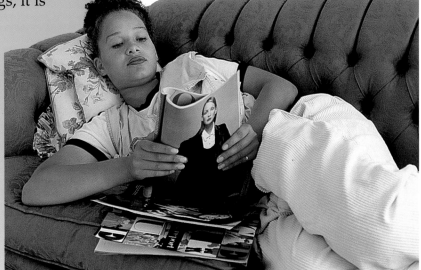

The war against illegal drugs

People in important positions often see illegal drugs from a particular point of view. Some policemen, politicians, and other people involved with the law may see drug users as criminals who have to be punished for breaking the law by being arrested, paying a fine, or going to prison. Some doctors see drug taking as a disease. If someone has problems with drugs they view him or her as not well and needing treatment with medicine in treatment centers.

Because illegal drug taking is so widespread all over the world, governments in many countries have declared a war on drugs. The action taken includes:

♦ keeping farmers from growing crops like coca, opium poppies, and marijuana
♦ finding out where the secret laboratories are that make drugs and closing them down
♦ keeping drugs from being transported from country to country by having customs officers in ports and airports to check on boats, planes, trucks, and people who might be carrying drugs
♦ arresting and putting into prison or fining people who supply drugs and people who use them

▲ *These young people from Zambia are acting in a play warning against the dangers of taking drugs.*

But is the war on illegal drugs working? The fact is that more and more drugs are available at cheaper prices, and more and more people are using them. Is it fair to punish individuals when drug use is part of a vast industry that stretches across continents?

Some people argue that the way to tackle the drug situation is to make the law stricter and punishments more harsh. They believe the courts should be harder on people who supply illegal drugs and put them in prison for life. They say that schools, TV and movies, newspapers, and magazines should push forward the message that all drugs are bad.

FACT:
The war on drugs costs the British government £1.4 billion in 1997. In the United States the government's drug control budget is more than $15 billion, four times more than was spent ten years earlier.
From *Forbidden Drugs*, Philip Robson, Oxford University Press

◀ *In many countries governments have declared a war on illegal drugs. These Colombian anti-drug squad officers are guarding an opium plantation.*

People who want to legalize drugs

Other people want all drugs to be made legal. These people think that people who take illegal drugs would be at less risk from illness or violence if these drugs were legal. People who wanted to take drugs would be able to have accurate information about different drugs and decide for themselves about drugs. Nor would people put themselves into dangerous situations to get illegal drugs. These people also think that people should not be punished for taking drugs on rare occasions. There are many arguments for legalizing drugs:

♦ Is it fair that some people are treated as criminals because they are involved in illegal drugs?

♦ Why should farmers who grow marijuana and coca be punished when farmers can grow grapes to make wine and tobacco without fear of the law?

♦ Is it right that people who have problems with drugs are put in prison when what they need is help?

♦ Shouldn't people be given the facts about drugs and left to make up their own minds whether they take them just as people choose whether to drink alcohol, smoke cigarettes, or eat too many fatty foods?

▲ *A member of the Cannabis Cultivator's Club in San Francisco. Members smoke marijuana, to help with illnesses such as cancer, arthritis, and multiple sclerosis.*

case study · case study · case study ·

Katy, a student, tried cannabis after seeing a band at the student union. She said "no" at first but later she asked to try it because she felt left out and wanted to join in with her friends.

After that, Katy began smoking marijuana with her boyfriend more regularly. It made her feel relaxed and happy. She enjoyed smoking it and sitting around playing cards and drinking coffee with her friends.

Katy has left college now and works all week but she still enjoys smoking cannabis on the weekend because it relaxes her. Katy doesn't feel like she is doing anything wrong even though she knows that smoking cannabis is against the law.

▲ *Many people in favor of legalizing drugs believe people should be given the facts and allowed to make up their own minds.*

▶ *Bolivian coca farmers protest against their crops being wiped out by the police and army. Should poor farmers who grow coca be punished when farmers can grow grapes to make wine perfectly legally?*

Making up your own mind about drugs

The fact is, there are two sides to every story—and many questions. Do people use drugs because they are poor and have few chances in life or does their drug use lead to poverty? Does taking drugs lead to people breaking the law? Or are people who break the law more likely to start taking illegal drugs? Is it better to be tough on drugs or is it more helpful to accept that we live in a drug-taking society and try to make drug use less harmful by giving people who take them information and help?

▼ *A young Vietnamese girl smiles as she shows off her new toy—a used syringe. Not knowing about the dangers of drugs can be as dangerous as the drugs themselves.*

"
"I don't think drugs should be decriminalized. I think making it easier would lead to more people having problems. Certainly, at the beginning of my drug-taking career, being able to buy lighter fuel and glue in the corner store made it easier."

Daisy, former heroin user
"

There are no simple answers to these questions. Some people think that giving young people information about drugs tempts them to try them for themselves. But not knowing about the risks of doing something can make it more dangerous, a bit like crossing the street without looking to see if there are any cars coming. Knowing the risks of drug taking can help you weigh the pros and cons for yourself. In this way you can protect yourself and stay safe.

"I think all recreational drugs should be legalized. Drugs, like Ecstasy, are around; kids are using them. To deny that is to stick our heads in the sand."

Chris Rea, rock star,
TRH Mirror 11.16.99

▲ *Ecstasy is taken by many young people who enjoy the effects it can give them. Knowing all the facts about drugs helps you make up your own mind about them.*

GLOSSARY

Addict
A drug user whose use of drugs is causing him or her problems in other areas of life.

Addiction
When someone's whole life revolves around getting and taking drugs.

Coke
Another name for the drug cocaine.

Dehydration
When the body does not have enough water.

Dependence
When someone feels he or she has to continue taking a drug to feel OK or to avoid feeling bad.

Depressants
Drugs that depress the nervous system.

Detoxification
The process of coming off drugs.

Hallucinogens
Drugs that cause hallucinations and change the way people see, hear, feel, or experience things.

HIV
The human immunodeficiency virus that causes AIDS.

Illicit
Something that is against the law.

Opiates
Drugs that are made from the opium poppy.

Over the counter
Drugs that you can buy at a drugstore without a prescription.

Overdose
Taking so much of a drug that the body or mind is unable to deal with its effects.

Problem drug use
When people's use of drugs is out of their control and is causing problems in other important areas of their life —with friends, family, work, money, and the law.

Psychological
Thoughts or feelings created in the mind—could be things that are not real or true.

Recreational drug use
When people use drugs for fun or in their spare time— Ecstacy and other "dance" drugs.

Sedatives
Drugs that stop anxiety.

Speed
Another name for amphetamines—a kind of drug that "speeds" people up and keeps them awake longer.

Stimulants
Drugs that increase the activity of the nervous system and make people feel energetic.

Tolerance
When the body gets used to a drug and needs more and more of it to produce the same effect.

Withdrawal
How the body reacts when a drug to which someone has become tolerant is no longer taken.

FURTHER INFORMATION

ORGANIZATIONS

There are many organizations providing information, help and advice on drugs. The organizations below can supply educational materials and resources. Information is also available on the Internet:

Alcohol and Drug Problems
Association of North America
1101 15th Street, NW
Suite 204
Washington, DC 20005

Alcoholics Anonymous
PO Box 459
Grand Central Station
New York, NY 10163
Tel: (212) 870 3400

MADD
(Mothers Against Drunk Driving)
511 E. John Carpenter Freeway
Irving, TX 75062

NCADD
(National Council on Alcoholism and
Drug Dependence)
12 West 21st Street
New York, NY 10010
Tel: (212) 206 6770

FURTHER READING

Barbour, Scott (ed.) *Alcohol!* (Opposing Viewpoints). San Diego, CA: Greenhaven Press, 1997.

Bayer, Linda N. *Amphetamines and Other Uppers* (Jr. Drug Awareness). Broomall, PA: Chelsea House, 1999.

Claypool, Jane. *Alcohol and You* (Impact). Danbury, CT: Franklin Watts, 1997.

Cohen, Daniel. "Prohibition: America Makes Alcohol Illegal." *Spotlight on American History*. Brookfield, CT: Millbrook Press, 1995.

Harris, Jacqueline. *Drugs and Disease* (Bodies in Crisis). New York: 21st Century Books, 1995.

Haughton, Emma. *A Right to Smoke* (Viewpoints). Danbury, CT: Franklin Watts, 1997.

Hyde, Margaret O. *Know About Smoking*. New York: Walker and Co., 1995.

Johnston, Marianne. *Let's Talk About Alcohol Abuse* (The Let's Talk About Library). New York: Rosen Publishing Group, 1997.

Lang, Alan R. "Alcohol: Teenage Drinking." *The Encyclopedia of Psychoactive Drugs*. New York: Chelsea House, 1992.

McGuire, Paula. *Alcohol* (Preteen Pressures). Austin, TX: Raintree Steck-Vaughn, 1998.

Pringle, Laurence. *Drinking: A Risky Business*. New York: William Morrow, 1997.

Robbins, Paul R. *Crack and Cocaine Drug Dangers* (Drug Dangers). Springfield, NJ: Enslow, 1999.

Ryan, Elizabeth A. *Straight Talk about Drugs and Alcohol* (Straight Talk). New York: Facts on File, 1995.

Seixas, Judith S. *Living with a Parent Who Drinks Too Much*. New York: William Morrow, 1983.

Websites

http://www.ncadd.org
American site with links to many other related sites.

http://www.alcoholconcern.org.uk
Home page for the UK organization Alcohol Concern.

http://www.nzdf.org
The New Zealand Drugs Foundation home page.

http://www.eurocare.org
A website with Europe-wide news, information, and discussions about alcohol.

INDEX